Student Edition

Journeys of Faith

Retracing the Faith-filled Steps of Great Bible Characters

Paul Chappell

First published in 2008 by Striving Together Publications, a
ministry of Lancaster Baptist Church, Lancaster, CA 93535.
Striving Together Publications is committed to providing tried,
trusted, and proven books that will further equip local churches
to carry out the Great Commission. Your comments and
suggestions are valued.

Striving Together Publications
4020 E. Lancaster Blvd.
Lancaster, CA 93535
800.201.7748

Cover design by Andrew Jones
Layout by Craig Parker
Edited by Pam Oslin and Danielle Mordh
Special thanks to our proofreaders.

ISBN 978-1-59894-070-1

Printed in the United States of America

Table of Contents

The Journey to Ararat

Key Verses

Genesis 6:1–9, 22

Lesson Overview

When God saw how wicked the people in the world had become, He was sorry that He had created them. Noah was the only one who walked with God. God warned Noah that He was going to destroy the world by a flood because of its wickedness, and He commanded him to build an ark for himself and his family. Noah obeyed without reservation. God gave him instructions for the ark, and he followed those instructions to the letter without questioning or reasoning with God. When the flood came, Noah and his family were safe in the ark. Because of Noah's obedience, God provided for and protected them.

Lesson Aim

Obedience to God is essential to a successful journey of faith, and we must be ready to obey God with a right spirit and willing heart.

Introduction

_____

_____

_____

I. The _____ for the Journey

A. *Corrupt* _____

B. *Corrupt* _____

II. _____ for the Journey

A. *Ready because of his* _____

B. *Ready because of his* _____

III. The _____ of the Journey

A. *Preservation of the* _____

GENESIS 6:14

14 Make thee an ark of gopher wood; rooms shalt thou make in the ark, and shalt pitch it within and without with pitch.

GENESIS 7:1

1   And the LORD said unto Noah, Come thou and all thy house into the ark; for thee have I seen righteous before me in this generation.

B. *Preservation of the* _____

C. *Preservation of the* _____

Conclusion

_____

_____

_____

MATTHEW 24:37–39

37 But as the days of Noe were, so shall also the coming of the Son of man be.

38 For as in the days that were before the flood they were eating and drinking, marrying and giving in marriage, until the day that Noe entered into the ark,

39 And knew not until the flood came, and took them all away; so shall also the coming of the Son of man be.

2 PETER 3:9

9 The Lord is not slack concerning his promise, as some men count slackness; but is longsuffering to us-ward, not willing that any should perish, but that all should come to repentance.

Study Questions

1. Why did God regret that He had created the world? What did He decide to do as a result?

2. In our text, what does the Hebrew word for "imagination" refer to? Explain what it means in the context of the passage we are studying.

3. What does a corrupt heart always lead to?

4. How can people today escape God's judgment?

5. How was Noah ready for his journey?

6. How did God preserve Noah as a result of his obedience?

7. List the pictures of salvation that we find in the story of Noah.

8.   Take a moment to identify areas in your life in which God is calling you to obedience. Are you willing and ready to obey? List the steps you must take to follow God in complete obedience to Him.

Memory Verse

2 PETER 3:9

9   *The Lord is not slack concerning his promise, as some men count slackness; but is longsuffering to us-ward, not willing that any should perish, but that all should come to repentance.*

The Journey to Mount Moriah

Key Verses
Genesis 22:1–19

Lesson Overview
God tested Abraham many times during his lifetime, but the greatest test came when God told Abraham to sacrifice his son Isaac. Abraham did not question or resist. He simply responded in obedience. When Abraham and his son reached Mount Moriah, he built an altar and laid Isaac upon it. As Abraham raised the knife, God knew that there was no end to Abraham's love and obedience. As a result, He provided a ram to sacrifice instead.

Lesson Aim
When God calls us to testing and sacrifice, our response should be one of immediate and faithful obedience, trusting Him to bring about His desired result in our lives.

Introduction

_____

_____

_____

HEBREWS 11:8–10

8   By faith Abraham, when he was called to go out into a place which he should after receive for an inheritance, obeyed; and he went out, not knowing whither he went.

9   By faith he sojourned in the land of promise, as in a strange country, dwelling in tabernacles with Isaac and Jacob, the heirs with him of the same promise:

10   For he looked for a city which hath foundations, whose builder and maker is God.

GENESIS 17:16–17

16   And I will bless her, and give thee a son also of her: yea, I will bless her, and she shall be a mother of nations; kings of people shall be of her.

17   Then Abraham fell upon his face, and laughed, and said in his heart, Shall a child be born unto him that is an hundred years old? and shall Sarah, that is ninety years old, bear?

I.   The _____ from the _____

A.   *A call to _____ (v. 1)*

1 PETER 1:7

7   That the trial of your faith, being much more precious than of gold that perisheth, though it be tried with fire, might be found unto praise and honour and glory at the appearing of Jesus Christ:

B. A call to _____ (v. 2)

GENESIS 15:5–6

5 And he brought him forth abroad, and said, Look now toward heaven, and tell the stars, if thou be able to number them: and he said unto him, So shall thy seed be.

6 And he believed in the LORD; and he counted it to him for righteousness.

HEBREWS 11:11–12

11 Through faith also Sarah herself received strength to conceive seed, and was delivered of a child when she was past age, because she judged him faithful who had promised.

12 Therefore sprang there even of one, and him as good as dead, so many as the stars of the sky in multitude, and as the sand which is by the sea shore innumerable.

II. The _____ of _____

A. _____ obedience (vv. 3–7)

ROMANS 1:17

17   For therein is the righteousness of God revealed from faith to faith: as it is written, The just shall live by faith.

HEBREWS 11:17–19

17   By faith Abraham, when he was tried, offered up Isaac: and he that had received the promises offered up his only begotten son,

18   Of whom it was said, That in Isaac shall thy seed be called:

19   Accounting that God was able to raise him up, even from the dead; from whence also he received him in a figure.

JOHN 19:17

17   And he bearing his cross went forth into a place called the place of a skull, which is called in the Hebrew Golgotha:

B. _____ obedience (v. 8)

HEBREWS 11:1–3

1   Now faith is the substance of things hoped for, the evidence of things not seen.

2   For by it the elders obtained a good report.

3   Through faith we understand that the worlds were framed by the word of God, so that things which are seen were not made of things which do appear.

HEBREWS 11:6

6   But without faith it is impossible to please him: for he that cometh to God must believe that he is, and that he is a rewarder of them that diligently seek him.

III. The _____ of _____

2 CORINTHIANS 1:3–4

3   Blessed be God, even the Father of our Lord Jesus Christ, the Father of mercies, and the God of all comfort;
4   Who comforteth us in all our tribulation, that we may be able to comfort them which are in any trouble, by the comfort wherewith we ourselves are comforted of God.

A. *Abraham prepares to* _____.

PHILIPPIANS 2:7–8

7   But made himself of no reputation, and took upon him the form of a servant, and was made in the likeness of men:
8   And being found in fashion as a man, he humbled himself, and became obedient unto death, even the death of the cross.

B. *God provides a* _____.

1 PETER 1:18–19

18   Forasmuch as ye know that ye were not redeemed with corruptible things, as silver and gold, from your vain conversation received by tradition from your fathers;

19   But with the precious blood of Christ, as of a lamb without blemish and without spot:

Conclusion

_____

_____

_____

Study Questions

1. According to Genesis 17:16–17, what did God promise to Abraham and Sarah?

2. On a scale of 1–10, rate your obedience to the Lord. Identify specific steps you can take to increase your level of obedience.

3. According to Hebrews 11:6, what one element is required in order to please God?

4. Has God required you to sacrifice something of significance in your life? How did you respond?

5. What does "Jehovah-Jireh" mean?

6. How did God provide for Abraham? How has God provided salvation for us?

7.   When Abraham began his journey to worship the Lord on Mount Moriah, he left his supplies and servants at the base of the mountain. Identify any hindrances that need to be left behind in your life and briefly describe what actions you will take to remove these hindrances to your worship.

8.   Are you trusting God to provide for your needs, as did Abraham? Take a moment and write a prayer to the Lord, expressing your confidence and trust in Him and thanking Him for being a trustworthy God.

Memory Verse

1 CORINTHIANS 10:13

13   There hath no temptation taken you but such as is common to man: but God is faithful, who will not suffer you to be tempted above that ye are able; but will with the temptation also make a way to escape, that ye may be able to bear it.

The Journey to the Palace

Key Verses
Exodus 1:1–22, Exodus 2:1–10

Lesson Overview
Pharaoh issued a decree that all baby boys born to the Hebrews in captivity were to be killed at birth. Amram and Jochebed were blessed with a baby boy, Moses. With love and courage, Moses' mother Jochebed placed Moses in a small waterproof basket and hid him in the Nile River. As he was hidden, the princess of Egypt came to the river. She heard the baby cry, sent her maids to find him, and took pity on the child. Moses' sister Miriam perceived what was happening and offered to find a nurse for the child. When the princess agreed, Miriam quickly ran to get Jochebed. The princess hired Jochebed, Moses' own mother, to raise this Hebrew baby for her. God protected Moses and provided his own mother to raise and train him to follow God's purposes for his life.

Lesson Aim
As Christians, we must trust the provision of the Lord and seek to fulfill the purposes given to us by God. As parents, we must protect our homes from the threat of evil and provide a Christ-honoring, loving environment for our children as we seek to raise them to discover God's unique purposes for their own lives.

Introduction

_____

_____

_____

Proverbs 31:10
10 Who can find a virtuous woman? for her price is far above rubies.

Proverbs 31:28
28 Her children arise up, and call her blessed; her husband also, and he praiseth her.

I. The _____ of Jochabed

Proverbs 1:8
8 My son, hear the instruction of thy father, and forsake not the law of thy mother:

A. From the _____ of evil

Hebrews 11:23
23 By faith Moses, when he was born, was hid three months of his parents, because they saw he was a proper child; and they were not afraid of the king's commandment.

B. From the _____ of Satan

1. Set boundaries.

Proverbs 4:1–2
1 Hear, ye children, the instruction of a father, and attend to know understanding.

2   For I give you good doctrine, forsake ye not my law.

2. Give warning
Proverbs 1:7

7   The fear of the Lord is the beginning of knowledge: but fools despise wisdom and instruction.

3. Set an example
2 Timothy 1:5

5   When I call to remembrance the unfeigned faith that is in thee, which dwelt first in thy grandmother Lois, and thy mother Eunice; and I am persuaded that in thee also.

4. Be wise to that which is good.
Romans 16:19

19   For your obedience is come abroad unto all men. I am glad therefore on your behalf: but yet I would have you wise unto that which is good, and simple concerning evil.

5. Teach the Word of God.
Deuteronomy 6:6–7

6   And these words, which I command thee this day, shall be in thine heart:

7   And thou shalt teach them diligently unto thy children, and shalt talk of them when thou sittest in thine house, and when thou walkest by the way, and when thou liest down, and when thou risest up.

6. Practice forgiveness.

EPHESIANS 4:32

32 And be ye kind one to another, tenderhearted, forgiving one another, even as God for Christ's sake hath forgiven you.

II. The _____ of the Lord

A. He provided a _____ for Moses.

1 TIMOTHY 5:8

8 But if any provide not for his own, and specially for those of his own house, he hath denied the faith, and is worse than an infidel.

B. He provides _____ for us.

EPHESIANS 6:4

4 And, ye fathers, provoke not your children to wrath: but bring them up in the nurture and admonition of the Lord.

PHILIPPIANS 4:9

9 Those things, which ye have both learned, and received, and heard, and seen in me, do: and the God of peace shall be with you.

III. The _____ of Moses

HEBREWS 11:24–26

24 By faith Moses, when he was come to years, refused to be called the son of Pharaoh's daughter;

25 Choosing rather to suffer affliction with the people of God, than to enjoy the pleasures of sin for a season;

26 Esteeming the reproach of Christ greater riches than the treasures in Egypt: for he had respect unto the recompense of the reward.

A. To identify with God's _____

HEBREWS 10:25

25 Not forsaking the assembling of ourselves together, as the manner of some is; but exhorting one another: and so much the more, as ye see the day approaching.

B. To separate from _____

DANIEL 1:8

8 But Daniel purposed in his heart that he would not defile himself with the portion of the king's meat, nor with the wine which he drank: therefore he requested of the prince of the eunuchs that he might not defile himself.

C. To wait on God's _____

Conclusion

_____

_____

_____

Study Questions

1. Following Jochebed's example, from what two types of snares are we to protect our children?

2. Describe one way God has provided for you when you trusted Him.

3. How is Satan attacking the Christian home today?

4. List the six ways we can protect our children.

5. According to Ephesians 6:4, how should we raise our children?

6. When it comes to identification, there is often a bent (in teens and adults alike) on acceptance from a peer or world system. List two sources from which you are tempted to seek acceptance (other than God and His people).

7. Using Hebrews 10:25 as a reference, identify one major way we can identify with God and His people.

Memory Verses

HEBREWS 11:24–26

24 By faith Moses, when he was come to years, refused to be called the son of Pharaoh's daughter;

25 Choosing rather to suffer affliction with the people of God, than to enjoy the pleasures of sin for a season;

26 Esteeming the reproach of Christ greater riches than the treasures in Egypt: for he had respect unto the recompense of the reward.

The Journey to Egypt

Key Verses

Genesis 37:1–10

Lesson Overview

In this day of confusion, Christians must understand the truth of God's Word regarding the doctrine of salvation. It is vitally important to equip every saint with scriptural truths which can be used in witnessing to coworkers, friends, and relatives. Through study, Christians can prepare to answer people's questions about God's saving grace, using the authority of the Bible.

Salvation points to the core of God's love—the gift of His Son on the Cross. The truths in this lesson enable Christians to make a difference with their lives each day.

Lesson Aim

We want to impress upon the student the importance of faith, faithfulness, and forgiveness as key essentials to a successful journey.

Introduction

_____

_____

_____

2 TIMOTHY 4:6–7

6 For I am now ready to be offered, and the time of my departure is at hand.

7 I have fought a good fight, I have finished my course, I have kept the faith:

I. A Journey of _____

GENESIS 35:1–5

1 And God said unto Jacob, Arise, go up to Bethel, and dwell there: and make there an altar unto God, that appeared unto thee when thou fleddest from the face of Esau thy brother.

2 Then Jacob said unto his household, and to all that were with him, Put away the strange gods that are among you, and be clean, and change your garments:

3 And let us arise, and go up to Bethel; and I will make there an altar unto God, who answered me in the day of my distress, and was with me in the way which I went.

4 And they gave unto Jacob all the strange gods which were in their hand, and all their earrings which were in their ears; and Jacob hid them under the oak which was by Shechem.

5 And they journeyed: and the terror of God was upon the cities that were round about them, and they did not pursue after the sons of Jacob.

A. Faith to _____ God's revelation

1 THESSALONIANS 2:13

13   For this cause also thank we God without ceasing, because, when ye received the word of God which ye heard of us, ye received it not as the word of men, but as it is in truth, the word of God, which effectually worketh also in you that believe.

B. Faith to _____ God's revelation

II. A Journey of _____

1 CORINTHIANS 4:2

2   Moreover it is required in stewards, that a man be found faithful.

A. When he was _____ by his brethren

GENESIS 37:11

11   And his brethren envied him; but his father observed the saying.

GENESIS 37:20

20   Come now therefore, and let us slay him, and cast him into some pit, and we will say, Some evil beast hath devoured him: and we shall see what will become of his dreams.

B. When he was _____ by his brethren

GENESIS 37:27–28

27   Come, and let us sell him to the Ishmeelites, and let not our hand be upon him; for he is our brother and our flesh. And his brethren were content.

28 Then there passed by Midianites merchantmen; and they drew and lifted up Joseph out of the pit, and sold Joseph to the Ishmeelites for twenty pieces of silver: and they brought Joseph into Egypt.

2 TIMOTHY 3:12
12 Yea, and all that will live godly in Christ Jesus shall suffer persecution.

C. *When he was* _____ *in Egypt*
GENESIS 39:2
2 And the LORD was with Joseph, and he was a prosperous man; and he was in the house of his master the Egyptian.

GENESIS 41:39–40
39 And Pharaoh said unto Joseph, Forasmuch as God hath shewed thee all this, there is none so discreet and wise as thou art:
40 Thou shalt be over my house, and according unto thy word shall all my people be ruled: only in the throne will I be greater than thou.

D. *When he was unjustly* _____
GENESIS 39:7–9
7 And it came to pass after these things, that his master's wife cast her eyes upon Joseph; and she said, Lie with me.
8 But he refused, and said unto his master's wife, Behold, my master wotteth not what is with me in the house, and he hath committed all that he hath to my hand;
9 There is none greater in this house than I; neither hath he kept back any thing from me but thee,

because thou art his wife: how then can I do this great wickedness, and sin against God?

1. Potiphar's wife attempted to seduce Joseph.

2 TIMOTHY 2:22

22 Flee also youthful lusts: but follow righteousness, faith, charity, peace, with them that call on the Lord out of a pure heart.

JAMES 1:12

12 Blessed is the man that endureth temptation: for when he is tried, he shall receive the crown of life, which the Lord hath promised to them that love him.

2. Joseph was faithful to God.

3. He was imprisoned for his faith.

GENESIS 39:20

20 And Joseph's master took him, and put him into the prison, a place where the king's prisoners were bound: and he was there in the prison.

4. God's mercy sustained him.

GENESIS 39:21

21 But the LORD was with Joseph, and shewed him mercy, and gave him favour in the sight of the keeper of the prison.

5. The Lord was with him.

GENESIS 39:23

23 *The keeper of the prison looked not to any thing that was under his hand; because the LORD was with him, and that which he did, the LORD made it to prosper.*

PROVERBS 16:7

7 *When a man's ways please the LORD, he maketh even his enemies to be at peace with him.*

1 CORINTHIANS 4:2

2 *Moreover it is required in stewards, that a man be found faithful.*

PHILIPPIANS 1:6

6 *Being confident of this very thing, that he which hath begun a good work in you will perform it until the day of Jesus Christ:*

III. A Journey of _____

HEBREWS 12:14–15

14 *Follow peace with all men, and holiness, without which no man shall see the Lord:*
15 *Looking diligently lest any man fail of the grace of God; lest any root of bitterness springing up trouble you, and thereby many be defiled;*

A. He _____ his brothers.

GENESIS 45:1–5

1 *Then Joseph could not refrain himself before all them that stood by him; and he cried, Cause every*

man to go out from me. And there stood no man with him, while Joseph made himself known unto his brethren.

2   And he wept aloud: and the Egyptians and the house of Pharaoh heard.

3   And Joseph said unto his brethren, I am Joseph; doth my father yet live? And his brethren could not answer him; for they were troubled at his presence.

4   And Joseph said unto his brethren, Come near to me, I pray you. And they came near. And he said, I am Joseph your brother, whom ye sold into Egypt.

5   Now therefore be not grieved, nor angry with yourselves, that ye sold me hither: for God did send me before you to preserve life.

1 John 1:9

9   If we confess our sins, he is faithful and just to forgive us our sins, and to cleanse us from all unrighteousness.

Ephesians 4:32

32   And be ye kind one to another, tenderhearted, forgiving one another, even as God for Christ's sake hath forgiven you.

B. He showed the _____ of God.
Genesis 42:25

25   Then Joseph commanded to fill their sacks with corn, and to restore every man's money into his sack, and to give them provision for the way: and thus did he unto them.

C. He showed the _____ of God.

GENESIS 45:7

7   And God sent me before you to preserve you a posterity in the earth, and to save your lives by a great deliverance.

ROMANS 8:28

28   And we know that all things work together for good to them that love God, to them who are the called according to his purpose.

D. He _____ on the Lord.

GENESIS 50:19–21

19   And Joseph said unto them, Fear not: for am I in the place of God?

20   But as for you, ye thought evil against me; but God meant it unto good, to bring to pass, as it is this day, to save much people alive.

21   Now therefore fear ye not: I will nourish you, and your little ones. And he comforted them, and spake kindly unto them.

Conclusion

_____

_____

_____

Study Questions

1. Joseph had faith to accept God's Word in the form of a dream. Today, God's Word is given to us in the Bible. Is there a command or truth that you are struggling to receive? Take a moment and write a prayer to the Lord, sincerely communicating your desire to accept and receive His direction in your life.

2. Joseph exercised faith to share God's Word with others. On a scale from 1–10, rate your personal soulwinning efforts. Now, create a brief action plan that will help increase your faith and efforts toward sharing the Gospel with others.

3. Name two things Joseph's brothers did to him.

4. According to 1 Corinthians 4:2, what is the one thing God requires of His stewards?

5. How could a promotion (to second-in-command over Egypt) have tempted Joseph to waver in his faithfulness to the Lord?

6. How did Joseph show his forgiveness to his brothers?

7. According to Genesis 42:25, how did Joseph show grace to his brothers?

8. How did Joseph demonstrate his focus on the Lord?

Memory Verse

1 CORINTHIANS 15:58

58 Therefore, my beloved brethren, be ye stedfast, unmoveable, always abounding in the work of the Lord, forasmuch as ye know that your labour is not in vain in the Lord.

The Journey to Sinai

Key Verses

Exodus 31:18–32:6, 30–33

Lesson Overview

God miraculously led the children of Israel out of the land of Egypt under the direction of Moses. While they journeyed through the wilderness, He sent daily miracles of provision, victory, and guidance. God settled the people at the foot of Mt. Sinai and called Moses up to the mountain where He communed with him forty days and forty nights. The children of Israel began to question what had happened to Moses. Beginning to doubt that he would ever return, they went to Aaron and demanded that he fashion an idol for them to worship. Aaron collected all the gold they brought from Egypt, made a golden calf, and God's people began to worship it.

Lesson Aim

This lesson provides a stark contrast between two types of people on their journey for the faith. Moses experienced a glorious journey, while Aaron and the children of Israel found themselves at a grievous juncture. Every Christian must desire to follow the example of Moses and to experience close communion with God.

Introduction

_____

_____

_____

I. A Glorious _____

DEUTERONOMY 34:10

10 And there arose not a prophet since in Israel like unto Moses, whom the LORD knew face to face,

A. *The* _____

EXODUS 3:4

4 And when the LORD saw that he turned aside to see, God called unto him out of the midst of the bush, and said, Moses, Moses. And he said, Here am I.

DEUTERONOMY 9:9–11

9 When I was gone up into the mount to receive the tables of stone, even the tables of the covenant which the LORD made with you, then I abode in the mount forty days and forty nights, I neither did eat bread nor drink water:

10 And the LORD delivered unto me two tables of stone written with the finger of God; and on them was written according to all the words, which the LORD spake with you in the mount out of the midst of the fire in the day of the assembly.

11 And it came to pass at the end of forty days and forty nights, that the LORD gave me the two tables of stone, even the tables of the covenant.

B. *The* _____

2 Peter 1:21

21 For the prophecy came not in old time by the will of man: but holy men of God spake as they were moved by the Holy Ghost.

Psalm 119:160

160 Thy word is true from the beginning: and every one of thy righteous judgments endureth for ever.

Hebrews 1:1–2

1 God, who at sundry times and in divers manners spake in time past unto the fathers by the prophets,
2 Hath in these last days spoken unto us by his Son, whom he hath appointed heir of all things, by whom also he made the worlds;

II. A Grievous _____

A. *The* _____ *of the people*

B. *The* _____ *of the people*

2 Corinthians 6:16

16 And what agreement hath the temple of God with idols? for ye are the temple of the living God; as God hath said, I will dwell in them, and walk in them; and I will be their God, and they shall be my people.

Exodus 32:17–18

17 And when Joshua heard the noise of the people as they shouted, he said unto Moses, There is a noise of war in the camp.

18   And he said, It is not the voice of them that shout for mastery, neither is it the voice of them that cry for being overcome: but the noise of them that sing do I hear.

1 CORINTHIANS 10:21–22

21   Ye cannot drink the cup of the Lord, and the cup of devils: ye cannot be partakers of the Lord's table, and of the table of devils.

22   Do we provoke the Lord to jealousy? are we stronger than he?

2 CORINTHIANS 6:15–17

15   And what concord hath Christ with Belial? or what part hath he that believeth with an infidel?

16   And what agreement hath the temple of God with idols? for ye are the temple of the living God; as God hath said, I will dwell in them, and walk in them; and I will be their God, and they shall be my people.

17   Wherefore come out from among them, and be ye separate, saith the Lord, and touch not the unclean thing; and I will receive you,

EXODUS 32:6

6   And they rose up early on the morrow, and offered burnt offerings, and brought peace offerings; and the people sat down to eat and to drink, and rose up to play.

1 CORINTHIANS 10:6–7

6   Now these things were our examples, to the intent we should not lust after evil things, as they also lusted.

7   Neither be ye idolaters, as were some of them; as it is written, The people sat down to eat and drink, and rose up to play.

III. A Gracious _____

A. The _____ of Moses

PHILIPPIANS 4:3

3   And I intreat thee also, true yokefellow, help those women which laboured with me in the gospel, with Clement also, and with other my fellowlabourers, whose names are in the book of life.

REVELATIONS 20:12–15

12   And I saw the dead, small and great, stand before God; and the books were opened: and another book was opened, which is the book of life: and the dead were judged out of those things which were written in the books, according to their works.

13   And the sea gave up the dead which were in it; and death and hell delivered up the dead which were in them: and they were judged every man according to their works.

14   And death and hell were cast into the lake of fire. This is the second death.

15   And whosoever was not found written in the book of life was cast into the lake of fire.

B. The _____ of Moses

HEBREWS 10:9–14

9   Then said he, Lo, I come to do thy will, O God. He taketh away the first, that he may establish the second.

10   By the which will we are sanctified through the offering of the body of Jesus Christ once for all.

11   And every priest standeth daily ministering and offering oftentimes the same sacrifices, which can never take away sins:

12   But this man, after he had offered one sacrifice for sins for ever, sat down on the right hand of God;

13   From henceforth expecting till his enemies be made his footstool.

14   For by one offering he hath perfected for ever them that are sanctified.

Conclusion

_____

_____

_____

Acts 4:12

12   Neither is there salvation in any other: for there is none other name under heaven given among men, whereby we must be saved.

Study Questions

1. According to Exodus 3:4, when did God commune with Moses for the first time?

2. Look up Deuteronomy 34:10 and Exodus 33:11. Describe the relationship between God and Moses.

3. Moses communed with God for forty days and nights without interruption. How is your communion with God? List three steps you can take this week to improve your relationship with God.

4. List the two indications that the children of Israel had come to a grievous juncture on their journey.

5. An idol is something that takes God's place in your heart. In the space provided, identify a potential idol in your life; then pause to pray that God will keep your heart free of idolatry on your journey for the faith.

6. What was Moses' problem, as recorded in the Scripture (Exodus 32:30–33) and how is it similar to the problem mankind faces today?

Memory Verse

2 CORINTHIANS 6:16

16 And what agreement hath the temple of God with idols? for ye are the temple of the living God; as God hath said, I will dwell in them, and walk in them; and I will be their God, and they shall be my people.

The Journey to the Promised Land

Key Verses

Joshua 1:1–9

Lesson Overview

Moses, the leader of Israel had died. Joshua, God's chosen leader had taken his place. He was the man who would lead the children of Israel into the Promised Land. We will study the life of Joshua and discover why God chose him to lead the children of Israel.

Lesson Aim

Many Christians feel inadequate when called upon by God to lead. God gives us the example of Joshua as he is placed in a position of leadership. We will look at how God prepared him and supplied everything he needed to do what God wanted him to do.

Introduction

_____

_____

_____

1 KINGS 18:21

21   *And Elijah came unto all the people, and said, How long halt ye between two opinions? if the LORD be God, follow him: but if Baal, then follow him. And the people answered him not a word.*

DEUTERONOMY 34:9

9   *And Joshua the son of Nun was full of the spirit of wisdom; for Moses had laid his hands upon him: and the children of Israel hearkened unto him, and did as the LORD commanded Moses.*

I.   Joshua's _____

PSALM 75:6–7

6   *For promotion cometh neither from the east, nor from the west, nor from the south,*

7   *But God is the judge: he putteth down one, and setteth up another.*

A.   *He was* _____.

EXODUS 17:8–13

8   *Then came Amalek, and fought with Israel in Rephidim.*

9   *And Moses said unto Joshua, Choose us out men, and go out, fight with Amalek: to morrow I will stand on the top of the hill with the rod of God in mine hand.*

10   *So Joshua did as Moses had said to him, and fought with Amalek: and Moses, Aaron, and Hur went up to the top of the hill.*

11   *And it came to pass, when Moses held up his hand, that Israel prevailed: and when he let down his hand, Amalek prevailed.*

12   *But Moses' hands were heavy; and they took a stone, and put it under him, and he sat thereon; and Aaron and Hur stayed up his hands, the one on the one side, and the other on the other side; and his hands were steady until the going down of the sun.*

13   *And Joshua discomfited Amalek and his people with the edge of the sword.*

B. He was a _____.

EXODUS 24:12–13

12   *And the LORD said unto Moses, Come up to me into the mount, and be there: and I will give thee tables of stone, and a law, and commandments which I have written; that thou mayest teach them.*

13   *And Moses rose up, and his minister Joshua: and Moses went up into the mount of God.*

MARK 10:45

45   *For even the Son of man came not to be ministered unto, but to minister, and to give his life a ransom for many.*

GALATIANS 5:13

13   *For, brethren, ye have been called unto liberty; only use not liberty for an occasion to the flesh, but by love serve one another.*

JUDGES 2:8

8   *And Joshua the son of Nun, the servant of the LORD, died, being an hundred and ten years old.*

C. He was _____.

EXODUS 24:18

18   And Moses went into the midst of the cloud, and gat him up into the mount. And Moses was in the mount forty days and forty nights.

EXODUS 32:15–17

15   And Moses turned, and went down from the mount, and the two tables of the testimony were in his hand: the tables were written on both their sides; on the one side and on the other were they written.

16   And the tables were the work of God, and the writing was the writing of God, graven upon the tables.

17   And when Joshua heard the noise of the people as they shouted, he said unto Moses, There is a noise of war in the camp.

PSALM 27:14

14   Wait on the LORD: be of good courage, and he shall strengthen thine heart: wait, I say, on the LORD.

D. He had a _____.

NUMBERS 14:6–10

6   And Joshua the son of Nun, and Caleb the son of Jephunneh, which were of them that searched the land, rent their clothes:

7   And they spake unto all the company of the children of Israel, saying, The land, which we passed through to search it, is an exceeding good land.

8   If the LORD delight in us, then he will bring us into this land, and give it us; a land which floweth with milk and honey.

9   Only rebel not ye against the LORD, neither fear ye the people of the land; for they are bread for us: their

defence is departed from them, and the LORD is with us: fear them not.

10   But all the congregation bade stone them with stones. And the glory of the LORD appeared in the tabernacle of the congregation before all the children of Israel.

PROVERBS 29:18

18   Where there is no vision, the people perish: but he that keepeth the law, happy is he.

II. Joshua's _____

A. *To provide* _____

JOSHUA 24:15

15   And if it seem evil unto you to serve the LORD, choose you this day whom ye will serve; whether the gods which your fathers served that were on the other side of the flood, or the gods of the Amorites, in whose land ye dwell: but as for me and my house, we will serve the LORD.

B. *To claim the* _____

JEREMIAH 29:11

11   For I know the thoughts that I think toward you, saith the LORD, thoughts of peace, and not of evil, to give you an expected end.

1 CORINTHIANS 15:57

57   But thanks be to God, which giveth us the victory through our Lord Jesus Christ.

ROMANS 8:36–37

36   As it is written, For thy sake we are killed all the day long; we are accounted as sheep for the slaughter.
37   Nay, in all these things we are more than conquerors through him that loved us.

III. Joshua's _____

A. *God's presence*
HEBREWS 13:5–6

5   Let your conversation be without covetousness; and be content with such things as ye have: for he hath said, I will never leave thee, nor forsake thee.
6   So that we may boldly say, The Lord is my helper, and I will not fear what man shall do unto me.

ZECHARIAH 4:6

6   Then he answered and spake unto me, saying, This is the word of the LORD unto Zerubbabel, saying, Not by might, nor by power, but by my spirit, saith the LORD of hosts.

B. *God's preserved Word*
MATTHEW 5:18

18   For verily I say unto you, Till heaven and earth pass, one jot or one tittle shall in no wise pass from the law, till all be fulfilled.

Conclusion

_____

_____

_____

Study Questions

1. What character traits in Joshua's life should we seek to emulate?

2. Take a moment to review Joshua's resume. Identify a characteristic in which you are weakest, and list an action that will help you strengthen your weakness in that area this week.

3. Joshua had two major responsibilities given to him from the Lord. What were they?

4. Identify a key area where you have a sphere of influence over others.

5. How is God using your life to influence others?

6. What resources has God promised to give you on your journey of influence?

7. God's Word is full of promises to the believer. Perhaps there is a certain promise that you have difficulty claiming. If so, list the promise below, and write out a prayer to the Lord, telling him that you will claim His promise in your life.

Memory Verse

2 PETER 3:18

18 But grow in grace, and in the knowledge of our Lord and Saviour Jesus Christ. To him be glory both now and for ever. Amen.

The Journey from Discouragement to Destiny

Key Verses

Judges 6:1–13

Lesson Overview

Israel was once again in bondage for their disobedience. God sent a prophet to call Israel to repentance, but they also needed a deliverer. God chose Gideon, an unlikely candidate in men's eyes, to deliver Israel from the Midianites. Gideon gathered Israel's army, and God thinned out the troops until the victory could only be a miracle of God. God used an unlikely general, and He received all the glory from the victory.

Lesson Aim

Many of us doubt our abilities and hide behind our feelings of inadequacy. We feel that God has a destiny for us to fulfill, but through our human reasoning, we do not see how we can reach that goal. That's what your journey for the faith is about. God knows what He has called you to do, and He knows exactly what qualities you need to fulfill that purpose. He promises to supply your every need and to strengthen your confidence in Him on your journey for the faith.

Introduction

_____

_____

_____

I. The _____ of Fear

JUDGES 6:22–23

22 *And when Gideon perceived that he was an angel of the LORD, Gideon said, Alas, O Lord GOD! for because I have seen an angel of the LORD face to face.*

23 *And the LORD said unto him, Peace be unto thee; fear not: thou shalt not die.*

A. *Fear leads to _____.*

B. *Fear leads to _____.*

PSALM 89:49

49 *Lord, where are thy former lovingkindnesses, which thou swarest unto David in thy truth?*

II. The _____ of Faith

ROMANS 10:17

17 *So then faith cometh by hearing, and hearing by the word of God.*

JUDGES 6:14–15

14 *And the LORD looked upon him, and said, Go in this thy might, and thou shalt save Israel from the hand of the Midianites: have not I sent thee?*

15   And he said unto him, Oh my Lord, wherewith shall I save Israel? behold, my family is poor in Manasseh, and I am the least in my father's house.

JUDGES 6:16

16   And the LORD said unto him, Surely I will be with thee, and thou shalt smite the Midianites as one man.

A.   *Faith is not* _____.

JUDGES 7:2–4

2   And the LORD said unto Gideon, The people that are with thee are too many for me to give the Midianites into their hands, lest Israel vaunt themselves against me, saying, Mine own hand hath saved me.

3   Now therefore go to, proclaim in the ears of the people, saying, Whosoever is fearful and afraid, let him return and depart early from mount Gilead. And there returned of the people twenty and two thousand; and there remained ten thousand.

4   And the LORD said unto Gideon, The people are yet too many; bring them down unto the water, and I will try them for thee there: and it shall be, that of whom I say unto thee, This shall go with thee, the same shall go with thee; and of whomsoever I say unto thee, This shall not go with thee, the same shall not go.

HEBREWS 11:32–34

32   And what shall I more say? for the time would fail me to tell of Gedeon, and of Barak, and of Samson, and of Jephthae; of David also, and Samuel, and of the prophets:

33   Who through faith subdued kingdoms, wrought righteousness, obtained promises, stopped the mouths of lions,

34   Quenched the violence of fire, escaped the edge of the sword, out of weakness were made strong, waxed valiant in fight, turned to flight the armies of the aliens.

B. Faith is _____.

HEBREW 11:6

6   But without faith it is impossible to please him: for he that cometh to God must believe that he is, and that he is a rewarder of them that diligently seek him.

JUDGES 7:8–9

8   So the people took victuals in their hand, and their trumpets: and he sent all the rest of Israel every man unto his tent, and retained those three hundred men: and the host of Midian was beneath him in the valley.

9   And it came to pass the same night, that the LORD said unto him, Arise, get thee down unto the host; for I have delivered it into thine hand.

ROMANS 8:31

31   What shall we then say to these things? If God be for us, who can be against us?

III. The _____ for the Faithful

A. God provides _____.

JUDGES 7:19–21

19   So Gideon, and the hundred men that were with him, came unto the outside of the camp in the beginning of the middle watch; and they had but newly set the watch: and they blew the trumpets, and brake the pitchers that were in their hands.

20 And the three companies blew the trumpets, and brake the pitchers, and held the lamps in their left hands, and the trumpets in their right hands to blow withal: and they cried, The sword of the LORD, and of Gideon.

21 And they stood every man in his place round about the camp: and all the host ran, and cried, and fled.

ISAIAH 55:8–9

8 For my thoughts are not your thoughts, neither are your ways my ways, saith the LORD.

9 For as the heavens are higher than the earth, so are my ways higher than your ways, and my thoughts than your thoughts.

JAMES 1:5

5 If any of you lack wisdom, let him ask of God, that giveth to all men liberally, and upbraideth not; and it shall be given him.

B. God provides _____.

JUDGES 8:1–4

1 And the men of Ephraim said unto him, Why hast thou served us thus, that thou calledst us not, when thou wentest to fight with the Midianites? And they did chide with him sharply.

2 And he said unto them, What have I done now in comparison of you? Is not the gleaning of the grapes of Ephraim better than the vintage of Abiezer?

3 God hath delivered into your hands the princes of Midian, Oreb and Zeeb: and what was I able to do in comparison of you? Then their anger was abated toward him, when he had said that.

4   And Gideon came to Jordan, and passed over, he, and the three hundred men that were with him, faint, yet pursuing them.

2 TIMOTHY 3:12
12   Yea, and all that will live godly in Christ Jesus shall suffer persecution.

2 CORINTHIANS 4:16–18
16   For which cause we faint not; but though our outward man perish, yet the inward man is renewed day by day.

17   For our light affliction, which is but for a moment, worketh for us a far more exceeding and eternal weight of glory;

18   While we look not at the things which are seen, but at the things which are not seen: for the things which are seen are temporal; but the things which are not seen are eternal.

Conclusion

_____

_____

_____

Study Questions

1. According to Judges 6:12, how did God see Gideon?

2. According to Judges 6:14–15, what were Gideon's objections to God's call?

3. What kind of effect does fear have on the life of a Christian?

4. Fear led to two specific results in Gideon's life. What were they?

5. God proved Gideon's faith by removing human instruments and military strength. In your life, are you depending on something other than the Lord? If so, what is it and what steps can you take to become more "God-confident"?

6. God promises His provision when we walk by faith. What two types of provision did God give to Gideon?

Memory Verse

2 TIMOTHY 1:7

7 For God hath not given us the spirit of fear; but of power, and of love, and of a sound mind.

The Journey to Jericho

Key Verses

Joshua 2:1–9

Lesson Overview

As Joshua and the children of Israel were claiming the land God had promised them, they came to a walled city called Jericho. This city had to be conquered if they were to possess the land. Before attacking, Joshua sent two spies into Jericho. The spies were soon within the city, mingling with the people and gathering information. The spies were found out and the city was on alert. When they turned into the home of a woman named Rahab, she hid them. Sending the soldiers on a futile search through the streets of the city, she went up to the roof and talked with the spies. She declared her belief that Israel's God was the one true God. Rahab asked for safety when they attacked the city. The spies made a pact with her that they would not destroy her family when they conquered Jericho.

Lesson Aim

Students should understand the change that salvation brings to the life of the believer. As new creatures in Christ, we must seek to live a life of faith demonstrated by our works.

Introduction

_____

_____

_____

I. The _____ of Rahab

A. *A reputation of* _____

Psalm 90:8

8   *Thou hast set* **our iniquities** *before thee, our secret sins in the light of thy countenance.*

Isaiah 59:2–4

2   *But* **your iniquities** *have separated between you and your God, and your sins have hid his face from you, that he will not hear.*

3   *For your hands are defiled with blood, and your fingers with iniquity; your lips have spoken lies, your tongue hath muttered perverseness.*

4   *None calleth for justice, nor any pleadeth for truth: they trust in vanity, and speak lies; they conceive mischief, and* **bring forth iniquity.**

B. *A reputation of* _____

Numbers 33:51–53

51   *…When ye are passed over Jordan into the land of Canaan;*

52   *Then ye shall drive out all the inhabitants of the land from before you, and destroy all their pictures, and destroy all their molten images, and quite pluck down all their high places:*

53 And ye shall dispossess the inhabitants of the land, and dwell therein: for I have given you the land to possess it.

EXODUS 20:3
3 Thou shalt have no other gods before me.

II. The _____ of Rahab

A. Her _____

1 TIMOTHY 2:4–5
4 Who will have all men to be saved, and to come unto the knowledge of the truth.
5 For there is one God, and one mediator between God and men, the man Christ Jesus;

EPHESIANS 4:17–18
17 This I say therefore, and testify in the Lord, that ye henceforth walk not as other Gentiles walk, in the vanity of their mind,
18 Having the understanding darkened, being alienated from the life of God through the ignorance that is in them, because of the blindness of their heart:

ACTS 9:4–6
4 And he fell to the earth, and heard a voice saying unto him, Saul, Saul, why persecutest thou me?
5 And he said, Who art thou, Lord? And the Lord said, I am Jesus whom thou persecutest: it is hard for thee to kick against the pricks.
6 And he trembling and astonished said, Lord, what wilt thou have me to do? And the Lord said unto him, Arise, and go into the city, and it shall be told thee what thou must do.

B. Her _____

JOSHUA 2:11

11   And as soon as we had heard these things, our hearts did melt, neither did there remain any more courage in any man, because of you: for the LORD your God, he is God in heaven above, and in earth beneath.

1 THESSALONIANS 1:9

9   For they themselves shew of us what manner of entering in we had unto you, and how ye turned to God from idols to serve the living and true God;

2 CORINTHIANS 5:17

17   Therefore if any man be in Christ, he is a new creature: old things are passed away; behold, all things are become new.

HEBREWS 11:31

31   By faith the harlot Rahab perished not with them that believed not, when she had received the spies with peace.

III. The _____ of Rahab

JAMES 2:17

17   Even so faith, if it hath not works, is dead, being alone.

A. To _____ the _____

JOSHUA 2:12–15

12   Now therefore, I pray you, swear unto me by the LORD, since I have shewed you kindness, that ye will also shew kindness unto my father's house, and give me a true token:

13   And that ye will save alive my father, and my mother, and my brethren, and my sisters, and all that they have, and deliver our lives from death.

14   And the men answered her, Our life for yours, if ye utter not this our business. And it shall be, when the LORD hath given us the land, that we will deal kindly and truly with thee.

15   Then she let them down by a cord through the window: for her house was upon the town wall, and she dwelt upon the wall.

JAMES 2:25

25   Likewise also was not Rahab the harlot justified by works, when she had received the messengers, and had sent them out another way?

B. To _____ her _____

JOSHUA 2:12–13

12   Now therefore, I pray you, swear unto me by the LORD, since I have shewed you kindness, that ye will also shew kindness unto my father's house, and give me a true token:

13   And that ye will save alive my father, and my mother, and my brethren, and my sisters, and all that they have, and deliver our lives from death.

JOSHUA 2:17–18

17   And the men said unto her, We will be blameless of this thine oath which thou hast made us swear.

18   Behold, when we come into the land, thou shalt bind this line of scarlet thread in the window which thou didst let us down by: and thou shalt bring thy

father, and thy mother, and thy brethren, and all thy father's household, home unto thee.

JOSHUA 6:22–23

22   But Joshua had said unto the two men that had spied out the country, Go into the harlot's house, and bring out thence the woman, and all that she hath, as ye sware unto her.

23   And the young men that were spies went in, and brought out Rahab, and her father, and her mother, and her brethren, and all that she had; and they brought out all her kindred, and left them without the camp of Israel.

JOSHUA 6:25

25   And Joshua saved Rahab the harlot alive, and her father's household, and all that she had; and she dwelleth in Israel even unto this day; because she hid the messengers, which Joshua sent to spy out Jericho.

EXODUS 12:13

13   And the blood shall be to you for a token upon the houses where ye are: and when I see the blood, I will pass over you, and the plague shall not be upon you to destroy you, when I smite the land of Egypt.

HEBREWS 9:22

22   And almost all things are by the law purged with blood; and without shedding of blood is no remission.

EPHESIANS 1:7

7   In whom we have redemption through his blood, the forgiveness of sins, according to the riches of his grace;

Conclusion

_____

_____

_____

JOSHUA 2:12

12 *Now therefore, I pray you, swear unto me by the LORD, since I have shewed you kindness, that ye will also shew kindness unto my father's house, and give me a true token:*

HEBREWS 11:31

31 *By faith the harlot Rahab perished not with them that believed not, when she had received the spies with peace.*

MATTHEW 1:5–6

5 *And Salmon begat Booz of Rachab; and Booz begat Obed of Ruth; and Obed begat Jesse;*

6 *And Jesse begat David the king; and David the king begat Solomon of her that had been the wife of Urias;*

Study Questions

1. Describe Rahab's reputation before she was saved.

2. An idol is anyone or anything that takes the place of God in your heart. Take a moment to search your heart and identify anything that may be an idol in your life. Write out a prayer to God, surrendering that idol to Him.

3. According to Joshua 2:9, what did Rahab realize or acknowledge?

4. How did Rahab demonstrate her repentance?

5. Write out 1 Thessalonians 1:9 in the space provided.

6. If our faith lacks works, how does the Bible describe it in James 2:17?

7. What two actions did Rahab perform that proved her faith in God?

8. Read Hebrews 11:31 and Matthew 1:5–6. According to these passages, what two blessings did Rahab receive?

Memory Verse

2 CORINTHIANS 5:17

17 Therefore if any man be in Christ, he is a new creature: old things are passed away; behold, all things are become new.

The Journey to Shiloh

Key Verses

1 Samuel 3:1–13

Lesson Overview

After earnestly praying for many years, Hannah bore a son, Samuel, and kept her promise to God. She gave Samuel back to God to serve Him in Shiloh. Because of his obedience and dedication in serving, God called Samuel to be the priest of Israel. Throughout his life, Samuel continued to obey and serve God. He faithfully declared righteousness and showed people the way of God.

Lesson Aim

To some, serving God has become something that is added to regular duties. For the Christian, serving God should be the umbrella under which every task is performed. Whether we are dictating a letter, balancing the books, nursing a patient, or changing a diaper, all is to be done as a service to God.

Introduction

_____

_____

_____

1 SAMUEL 1:11

11 And she vowed a vow, and said, O LORD of hosts, if thou wilt indeed look on the affliction of thine handmaid, and remember me, and not forget thine handmaid, but wilt give unto thine handmaid a man child, then I will give him unto the LORD all the days of his life, and there shall no razor come upon his head.

I. The _____ of Samuel

A. The _____ of Samuel

B. The _____ of God

1 SAMUEL 3:12–14

12 In that day I will perform against Eli all things which I have spoken concerning his house: when I begin, I will also make an end.

13 For I have told him that I will judge his house for ever for the iniquity which he knoweth; because his sons made themselves vile, and he restrained them not.

14 And therefore I have sworn unto the house of Eli, that the iniquity of Eli's house shall not be purged with sacrifice nor offering for ever.

2 TIMOTHY 2:20–21

20   But in a great house there are not only vessels of gold and of silver, but also of wood and of earth; and some to honour, and some to dishonour.

21   If a man therefore purge himself from these, he shall be a vessel unto honour, sanctified, and meet for the master's use, and prepared unto every good work.

1 SAMUEL 2:22, 26

22   Now Eli was very old, and heard all that his sons did unto all Israel; and how they lay with the women that assembled at the door of the tabernacle of the congregation.

26   And the child Samuel grew on, and was in favour both with the LORD, and also with men.

1 SAMUEL 3:17–19

17   And he said, What is the thing that the LORD hath said unto thee? I pray thee hide it not from me: God do so to thee, and more also, if thou hide any thing from me of all the things that he said unto thee.

18   And Samuel told him every whit, and hid nothing from him. And he said, It is the LORD: let him do what seemeth him good.

19   And Samuel grew, and the LORD was with him, and did let none of his words fall to the ground.

DEUTERONOMY 18:20–22

20   But the prophet, which shall presume to speak a word in my name, which I have not commanded him to speak, or that shall speak in the name of other gods, even that prophet shall die.

21   And if thou say in thine heart, How shall we know the word which the LORD hath not spoken?

22 *When a prophet speaketh in the name of the Lord, if the thing follow not, nor come to pass, that is the thing which the Lord hath not spoken, but the prophet hath spoken it presumptuously: thou shalt not be afraid of him.*

1 CORINTHIANS 15:58

58 *Therefore, my beloved brethren, be ye stedfast, unmoveable, always abounding in the work of the Lord, forasmuch as ye know that your labour is not in vain in the Lord.*

II. The _____ of the People

A. A _____ *covenant*

1 SAMUEL 7:2–3

2 *And it came to pass, while the ark abode in Kirjathjearim, that the time was long; for it was twenty years: and all the house of Israel lamented after the Lord.*

3 *And Samuel spake unto all the house of Israel, saying, If ye do return unto the Lord with all your hearts, then put away the strange gods and Ashtaroth from among you, and prepare your hearts unto the Lord, and serve him only: and he will deliver you out of the hand of the Philistines.*

JUDGE 13:1

1 *And the children of Israel did evil again in the sight of the Lord; and the Lord delivered them into the hand of the Philistines forty years.*

B. A _____ for help

1 SAMUEL 7:8–10

8   And the children of Israel said to Samuel, Cease not to cry unto the LORD our God for us, that he will save us out of the hand of the Philistines.

9   And Samuel took a sucking lamb, and offered it for a burnt offering wholly unto the LORD: and Samuel cried unto the LORD for Israel; and the LORD heard him.

10   And as Samuel was offering up the burnt offering, the Philistines drew near to battle against Israel: but the LORD thundered with a great thunder on that day upon the Philistines, and discomfited them; and they were smitten before Israel.

PSALM 66:18

18   If I regard iniquity in my heart, the Lord will not hear me:

1 SAMUEL 7:12

12   Then Samuel took a stone, and set it between Mizpeh and Shen, and called the name of it Ebenezer, saying, Hitherto hath the LORD helped us.

PSALM 18:2

2   The LORD is my rock, and my fortress, and my deliverer; my God, my strength, in whom I will trust; my buckler, and the horn of my salvation, and my high tower.

III. The _____ of Samuel

1 SAMUEL 8:19–20

19 Nevertheless the people refused to obey the voice of Samuel; and they said, Nay; but we will have a king over us;

20 That we also may be like all the nations; and that our king may judge us, and go out before us, and fight our battles.

A. The people _____ the hand of the Lord.

1 SAMUEL 12:8–9

8 When Jacob was come into Egypt, and your fathers cried unto the LORD, then the LORD sent Moses and Aaron, which brought forth your fathers out of Egypt, and made them dwell in this place.

9 And when they forgat the LORD their God, he sold them into the hand of Sisera, captain of the host of Hazor, and into the hand of the Philistines, and into the hand of the king of Moab, and they fought against them.

1 SAMUEL 12:12

12 And when ye saw that Nahash the king of the children of Ammon came against you, ye said unto me, Nay; but a king shall reign over us: when the LORD your God was your king.

B. Saul _____ the order of the Lord.

1 SAMUEL 13:8–12

8 And he tarried seven days, according to the set time that Samuel had appointed: but Samuel came not to Gilgal; and the people were scattered from him.

9 And Saul said, Bring hither a burnt offering to me, and peace offerings. And he offered the burnt offering.

10   And it came to pass, that as soon as he had made an end of offering the burnt offering, behold, Samuel came; and Saul went out to meet him, that he might salute him.

11   And Samuel said, What hast thou done? And Saul said, Because I saw that the people were scattered from me, and that thou camest not within the days appointed, and that the Philistines gathered themselves together at Michmash;

12   Therefore said I, The Philistines will come down now upon me to Gilgal, and I have not made supplication unto the LORD: I forced myself therefore, and offered a burnt offering.

ACTS 4:12

12   Neither is there salvation in any other: for there is none other name under heaven given among men, whereby we must be saved.

1 SAMUEL 13:13–14

13   And Samuel said to Saul, Thou hast done foolishly: thou hast not kept the commandment of the LORD thy God, which he commanded thee: for now would the LORD have established thy kingdom upon Israel for ever.

14   But now thy kingdom shall not continue: the LORD hath sought him a man after his own heart, and the LORD hath commanded him to be captain over his people, because thou hast not kept that which the LORD commanded thee.

PROVERBS 14:12

12   There is a way which seemeth right unto a man, but the end thereof are the ways of death.

Conclusion

Study Questions

1. What characteristic is evident in the lives of both Hannah and Samuel?

2. God had two primary purposes for Samuel which he accomplished throughout his life. What were they?

3. One of God's purposes for Samuel was to speak His words, not letting one fall to the ground. Are you faithful to tell others of God's plan of salvation? What can you do this week to share His Gospel message with those around you?

4. As seen in our lesson, what must we do before we call upon the Lord for help?

5. Write out Psalm 66:18 in the space provided below. If there is any iniquity in your heart, take a moment right now to confess it to the Lord.

6. Briefly describe Saul's actions that replaced the order of the Lord.

7. Name an obvious example of the children of Israel refusing the hand of the Lord.

8. God called Samuel to a lifetime of service for Him. Has God called you to a particular area of service? Are you performing it out of a heart of love for Him? Take a moment and write a quick evaluation of your service to God in light of Samuel's sacrificial service in Shiloh and throughout his life.

Memory Verses

1 PETER 1:14–16

14 As obedient children, not fashioning yourselves according to the former lusts in your ignorance:

15 But as he which hath called you is holy, so be ye holy in all manner of conversation;

16 Because it is written, Be ye holy; for I am holy.

The Journey to the Valley of Elah

Key Verse

1 Samuel 16:1–13

Lesson Overview

David was a young lad who obeyed God completely. He was a man after God's own heart, and God chose him to be the next king of Israel. God took David on a journey that caused his confidence in Him to grow. His most well known battle was with Goliath, the giant Philistine in the Valley of Elah. Young David was the instrument God used to defeat the giant and give glory to God.

Lesson Aim

Battles in the Christian life are inevitable, but as we cultivate hearts for God, we are given a purpose. We are able to live for a holy cause. Along the course of our journeys, God will prepare us for these battles. Then, he will give us the power to prevail for His glory!

Introduction

_____

_____

_____

1 SAMUEL 13:6–7

6 When the men of Israel saw that they were in a strait, (for the people were distressed,) then the people did hide themselves in caves, and in thickets, and in rocks, and in high places, and in pits.

7 And some of the Hebrews went over Jordan to the land of Gad and Gilead. As for Saul, he was yet in Gilgal, and all the people followed him trembling.

1 SAMUEL 13:13–14

13 And Samuel said to Saul, Thou hast done foolishly: thou hast not kept the commandment of the LORD thy God, which he commanded thee: for now would the LORD have established thy kingdom upon Israel for ever.

14 But now thy kingdom shall not continue: the LORD hath sought him a man after his own heart, and the LORD hath commanded him to be captain over his people, because thou hast not kept that which the LORD commanded thee.

1 SAMUEL 15:26

26 And Samuel said unto Saul, I will not return with thee: for thou hast rejected the word of the LORD, and the LORD hath rejected thee from being king over Israel.

I. David's _____

A. The _____ of David's calling

1 SAMUEL 16:1

1 And the LORD said unto Samuel, How long wilt thou mourn for Saul, seeing I have rejected him from reigning over Israel? fill thine horn with oil, and go, I will send thee to Jesse the Bethlehemite: for I have provided me a king among his sons.

1 SAMUEL 8:5

5 And said unto him, Behold, thou art old, and thy sons walk not in thy ways: now make us a king to judge us like all the nations.

1 SAMUEL 15:11

11 It repenteth me that I have set up Saul to be king: for he is turned back from following me, and hath not performed my commandments. And it grieved Samuel; and he cried unto the LORD all night.

1 SAMUEL 13:14

14 But now thy kingdom shall not continue: the LORD hath sought him a man after his own heart, and the LORD hath commanded him to be captain over his people, because thou hast not kept that which the LORD commanded thee.

B. The _____ of David's calling

ACTS 13:22

22 And when he had removed him, he raised up unto them David to be their king; to whom also he gave testimony, and said, I have found David the son of

Jesse, a man after mine own heart, which shall fulfil all my will.

1 SAMUEL 16:18

18 *Then answered one of the servants, and said, Behold, I have seen a son of Jesse the Bethlehemite, that is cunning in playing, and a mighty valiant man, and a man of war, and prudent in matters, and a comely person, and the LORD is with him.*

EPHESIANS 5:18

18 *And be not drunk with wine, wherein is excess; but be filled with the Spirit;*

ACTS 1:8

8 *But ye shall receive power, after that the Holy Ghost is come upon you: and ye shall be witnesses unto me both in Jerusalem, and in all Judaea, and in Samaria, and unto the uttermost part of the earth.*

II. David's _____

A. *His cause was for the _____.*

1 SAMUEL 17:1–8

1 *Now the Philistines gathered together their armies to battle, and were gathered together at Shochoh, which belongeth to Judah, and pitched between Shochoh and Azekah, in Ephesdammim.*

2 *And Saul and the men of Israel were gathered together, and pitched by the valley of Elah, and set the battle in array against the Philistines.*

3   And the Philistines stood on a mountain on the one side, and Israel stood on a mountain on the other side: and there was a valley between them.

4   And there went out a champion out of the camp of the Philistines, named Goliath, of Gath, whose height was six cubits and a span.

5   And he had an helmet of brass upon his head, and he was armed with a coat of mail; and the weight of the coat was five thousand shekels of brass.

6   And he had greaves of brass upon his legs, and a target of brass between his shoulders.

7   And the staff of his spear was like a weaver's beam; and his spear's head weighed six hundred shekels of iron: and one bearing a shield went before him.

8   And he stood and cried unto the armies of Israel, and said unto them, Why are ye come out to set your battle in array? am not I a Philistine, and ye servants to Saul? choose you a man for you, and let him come down to me.

1 Samuel 17:16

16   And the Philistine drew near morning and evening, and presented himself forty days.

1 Samuel 17:21–29

21   For Israel and the Philistines had put the battle in array, army against army.

22   And David left his carriage in the hand of the keeper of the carriage, and ran into the army, and came and saluted his brethren.

23   And as he talked with them, behold, there came up the champion, the Philistine of Gath, Goliath by name, out of the armies of the Philistines, and spake according to the same words: and David heard them.

24 And all the men of Israel, when they saw the man, fled from him, and were sore afraid.

25 And the men of Israel said, Have ye seen this man that is come up? surely to defy Israel is he come up: and it shall be, that the man who killeth him, the king will enrich him with great riches, and will give him his daughter, and make his father's house free in Israel.

26 And David spake to the men that stood by him, saying, What shall be done to the man that killeth this Philistine, and taketh away the reproach from Israel? for who is this uncircumcised Philistine, that he should defy the armies of the living God?

27 And the people answered him after this manner, saying, So shall it be done to the man that killeth him.

28 And Eliab his eldest brother heard when he spake unto the men; and Eliab's anger was kindled against David, and he said, Why camest thou down hither? and with whom hast thou left those few sheep in the wilderness? I know thy pride, and the naughtiness of thine heart; for thou art come down that thou mightest see the battle.

29 And David said, What have I now done? Is there not a cause?

2 TIMOTHY 1:11–12

11 Whereunto I am appointed a preacher, and an apostle, and a teacher of the Gentiles.

12 For the which cause I also suffer these things: nevertheless I am not ashamed: for I know whom I have believed, and am persuaded that he is able to keep that which I have committed unto him against that day.

B. His cause was _____. (v. 17:28)

1 Samuel 17:31–33

31 And when the words were heard which David spake, they rehearsed them before Saul: and he sent for him.

32 And David said to Saul, Let no man's heart fail because of him; thy servant will go and fight with this Philistine.

33 And Saul said to David, Thou art not able to go against this Philistine to fight with him: for thou art but a youth, and he a man of war from his youth.

III. David's _____

A. David's _____ **for battle**

1 Samuel 17:33–37

33 And Saul said to David, Thou art not able to go against this Philistine to fight with him: for thou art but a youth, and he a man of war from his youth.

34 And David said unto Saul, Thy servant kept his father's sheep, and there came a lion, and a bear, and took a lamb out of the flock:

35 And I went out after him, and smote him, and delivered it out of his mouth: and when he arose against me, I caught him by his beard, and smote him, and slew him.

36 Thy servant slew both the lion and the bear: and this uncircumcised Philistine shall be as one of them, seeing he hath defied the armies of the living God.

37 David said moreover, The Lord that delivered me out of the paw of the lion, and out of the paw of the bear, he will deliver me out of the hand of this

Philistine. And Saul said unto David, Go, and the LORD *be with thee.*

1 SAMUEL 17:38–40

38 And Saul armed David with his armour, and he put an helmet of brass upon his head; also he armed him with a coat of mail.

39 And David girded his sword upon his armour, and he assayed to go; for he had not proved it. And David said unto Saul, I cannot go with these; for I have not proved them. And David put them off him.

40 And he took his staff in his hand, and chose him five smooth stones out of the brook, and put them in a shepherd's bag which he had, even in a scrip; and his sling was in his hand: and he drew near to the Philistine.

1 CORINTHIANS 1:27–29

27 But God hath chosen the foolish things of the world to confound the wise; and God hath chosen the weak things of the world to confound the things which are mighty;

28 And base things of the world, and things which are despised, hath God chosen, yea, and things which are not, to bring to nought things that are:

29 That no flesh should glory in his presence.

B. David's _____ *in battle*

PHILIPPIANS 4:13

13 I can do all things through Christ which strengtheneth me.

1 SAMUEL 17:45–47

45 Then said David to the Philistine, Thou comest to me with a sword, and with a spear, and with a shield:

but I come to thee in the name of the LORD of hosts, the God of the armies of Israel, whom thou hast defied.

46   This day will the LORD deliver thee into mine hand; and I will smite thee, and take thine head from thee; and I will give the carcases of the host of the Philistines this day unto the fowls of the air, and to the wild beasts of the earth; that all the earth may know that there is a God in Israel.

47   And all this assembly shall know that the LORD saveth not with sword and spear: for the battle is the LORD's, and he will give you into our hands.

Zechariah 4:6

6   Then he answered and spake unto me, saying, This is the word of the LORD unto Zerubbabel, saying, Not by might, nor by power, but by my spirit, saith the LORD of hosts.

C. David's _____ **in battle**

1 Samuel 17:48–51

48   And it came to pass, when the Philistine arose, and came and drew nigh to meet David, that David hasted, and ran toward the army to meet the Philistine.

49   And David put his hand in his bag, and took thence a stone, and slang it, and smote the Philistine in his forehead, that the stone sunk into his forehead; and he fell upon his face to the earth.

50   So David prevailed over the Philistine with a sling and with a stone, and smote the Philistine, and slew him; but there was no sword in the hand of David.

51   Therefore David ran, and stood upon the Philistine, and took his sword, and drew it out of the sheath thereof, and slew him, and cut off his head therewith.

And when the Philistines saw their champion was dead, they fled.

Psalm 115:1–3

1   Not unto us, O Lord, not unto us, but unto thy name give glory, for thy mercy, and for thy truth's sake.

2   Wherefore should the heathen say, Where is now their God?

3   But our God is in the heavens: he hath done whatsoever he hath pleased.

Matthew 19:26

26 But Jesus beheld them, and said unto them, With men this is impossible; but with God all things are possible.

Conclusion

_____

_____

_____

Isaiah 11:1–3

1   And there shall come forth a rod out of the stem of Jesse, and a Branch shall grow out of his roots:

2   And the spirit of the Lord shall rest upon him, the spirit of wisdom and understanding, the spirit of counsel and might, the spirit of knowledge and of the fear of the Lord;

3   And shall make him of quick understanding in the fear of the Lord: and he shall not judge after the sight of his eyes, neither reprove after the hearing of his ears:

Study Questions

1. According to Acts 13:22, how was David's heart described?

2. As Samuel looked at Jesse's sons, which one did he think would be the next king?

3. According to 1 Samuel 16:7, when God looks at us, what does He see?

4. In the Old Testament, what did the anointing of oil symbolize?

5. Read 2 Timothy 1:11–12. Here, Paul states his call and his cause. Briefly explain how these verses can also describe the calling and cause of David.

6. Name two people who challenged David's cause.

7. What experiences prepared David for battle against Goliath?

Memory Verse

HEBREWS 4:16

16 *Let us therefore come boldly unto the throne of grace, that we may obtain mercy, and find grace to help in time of need.*

The Journey to Zion

Key Verses

1 Samuel 18:1–9; 2 Samuel 11–12

Lesson Overview

As Christians, we will face trials and temptations on our journeys of faith. David faced an intense trial for an extended period when King Saul was trying to kill him. His response to the trial is an example for us to follow. Later, when David became king, he faced a great temptation and chose to sin. Throughout this lesson, we examine David's life, the consequences of his sin, and the steps he followed to restore his fellowship with a holy God.

Lesson Aim

We want to impress upon the student the importance of staying focused on God during times of trial and fleeing Satan during times of temptation. When we fall during one of these times, we can experience triumph when we confess our sin to the Lord.

Introduction

_____

_____

_____

I. David's Great _____
1 Samuel 18:10–12

10 And it came to pass on the morrow, that the evil spirit from God came upon Saul, and he prophesied in the midst of the house: and David played with his hand, as at other times: and there was a javelin in Saul's hand.

11 And Saul cast the javelin; for he said, I will smite David even to the wall with it. And David avoided out of his presence twice.

12 And Saul was afraid of David, because the LORD was with him, and was departed from Saul.

A. The _____ for the trial
1 Samuel 18:16

16 But all Israel and Judah loved David, because he went out and came in before them.

B. The _____ to the trial
1 Samuel 19:10

10 And Saul sought to smite David even to the wall with the javelin; but he slipped away out of Saul's presence, and he smote the javelin into the wall: and David fled, and escaped that night.

1 SAMUEL 22:1–2

1   David therefore departed thence, and escaped to the cave Adullam: and when his brethren and all his father's house heard it, they went down thither to him.

2   And every one that was in distress, and every one that was in debt, and every one that was discontented, gathered themselves unto him; and he became a captain over them: and there were with him about four hundred men.

1 SAMUEL 27:1–2

1   And David said in his heart, I shall now perish one day by the hand of Saul: there is nothing better for me than that I should speedily escape into the land of the Philistines; and Saul shall despair of me, to seek me any more in any coast of Israel: so shall I escape out of his hand.

2   And David arose, and he passed over with the six hundred men that were with him unto Achish, the son of Maoch, king of Gath.

C. His _____ in the trial

1 SAMUEL 30:6

6   And David was greatly distressed; for the people spake of stoning him, because the soul of all the people was grieved, every man for his sons and for his daughters: but David encouraged himself in the LORD his God.

1 CORINTHIANS 10:13

13   There hath no temptation taken you but such as is common to man: but God is faithful, who will not suffer you to be tempted above that ye are able; but

will with the temptation also make a way to escape, that ye may be able to bear it.

II. David's Great _____

2 SAMUEL 5:3–4

3   So all the elders of Israel came to the king to Hebron; and king David made a league with them in Hebron before the LORD: and they anointed David king over Israel.

4   David was thirty years old when he began to reign, and he reigned forty years.

2 SAMUEL 11:1–5

1   And it came to pass, after the year was expired, at the time when kings go forth to battle, that David sent Joab, and his servants with him, and all Israel; and they destroyed the children of Ammon, and besieged Rabbah. But David tarried still at Jerusalem.

2   And it came to pass in an eveningtide, that David arose from off his bed, and walked upon the roof of the king's house: and from the roof he saw a woman washing herself; and the woman was very beautiful to look upon.

3   And David sent and enquired after the woman. And one said, Is not this Bathsheba, the daughter of Eliam, the wife of Uriah the Hittite?

4   And David sent messengers, and took her; and she came in unto him, and he lay with her; for she was purified from her uncleanness: and she returned unto her house.

5   And the woman conceived, and sent and told David, and said, I am with child.

A. *David's* _____

B. *David's* _____

    1. His _____

    2. His _____

1 PETER 5:8

8   Be sober, be vigilant; because your adversary the devil, as a roaring lion, walketh about, seeking whom he may devour:

    3. His _____

2 SAMUEL 11:15–17

15   And he wrote in the letter, saying, Set ye Uriah in the forefront of the hottest battle, and retire ye from him, that he may be smitten, and die.

16   And it came to pass, when Joab observed the city, that he assigned Uriah unto a place where he knew that valiant men were.

17   And the men of the city went out, and fought with Joab: and there fell some of the people of the servants of David; and Uriah the Hittite died also.

2 SAMUEL 11:26–27

26   And when the wife of Uriah heard that Uriah her husband was dead, she mourned for her husband.

27   And when the mourning was past, David sent and fetched her to his house, and she became his wife, and bare him a son. But the thing that David had done displeased the LORD.

C. David's _____

2 SAMUEL 12:14

14   Howbeit, because by this deed thou hast given great occasion to the enemies of the LORD to blaspheme, the child also that is born unto thee shall surely die.

GALATIANS 6:7–8

7   Be not deceived; God is not mocked: for whatsoever a man soweth, that shall he also reap.

8   For he that soweth to his flesh shall of the flesh reap corruption; but he that soweth to the Spirit shall of the Spirit reap life everlasting.

III. David's _____

A. A righteous _____

2 SAMUEL 12:1–6

1   And the LORD sent Nathan unto David. And he came unto him, and said unto him, There were two men in one city; the one rich, and the other poor.

2   The rich man had exceeding many flocks and herds:

3   But the poor man had nothing, save one little ewe lamb, which he had bought and nourished up: and it grew up together with him, and with his children; it did eat of his own meat, and drank of his own cup, and lay in his bosom, and was unto him as a daughter.

4   And there came a traveller unto the rich man, and he spared to take of his own flock and of his own herd, to dress for the wayfaring man that was come unto him; but took the poor man's lamb, and dressed it for the man that was come to him.

5 And David's anger was greatly kindled against the man; and he said to Nathan, As the LORD liveth, the man that hath done this thing shall surely die:

6 And he shall restore the lamb fourfold, because he did this thing, and because he had no pity.

2 SAMUEL 12:7–9

7 And Nathan said to David, **Thou art the man.** Thus saith the LORD God of Israel, I anointed thee king over Israel, and I delivered thee out of the hand of Saul;

8 And I gave thee thy master's house, and thy master's wives into thy bosom, and gave thee the house of Israel and of Judah; and if that had been too little, I would moreover have given unto thee such and such things.

9 Wherefore hast thou despised the commandment of the LORD, to do evil in his sight? thou hast killed Uriah the Hittite with the sword, and hast taken his wife to be thy wife, and hast slain him with the sword of the children of Ammon.

B. A real _____

2 SAMUEL 12:13–14

13 And David said unto Nathan, I have sinned against the LORD. And Nathan said unto David, The LORD also hath put away thy sin; thou shalt not die.

14 Howbeit, because by this deed thou hast given great occasion to the enemies of the LORD to blaspheme, the child also that is born unto thee shall surely die.

PSALM 51:3–4

3 For I acknowledge my transgressions: and my sin is ever before me.

4   *Against thee, thee only, have I sinned, and done this evil in thy sight: that thou mightest be justified when thou speakest, and be clear when thou judgest.*

C. A restored _____

2 SAMUEL 22:1–4

1   *And David spake unto the LORD the words of this song in the day that the LORD had delivered him out of the hand of all his enemies, and out of the hand of Saul:*

2   *And he said, The LORD is my rock, and my fortress, and my deliverer;*

3   *The God of my rock; in him will I trust: he is my shield, and the horn of my salvation, my high tower, and my refuge, my saviour; thou savest me from violence.*

4   *I will call on the LORD, who is worthy to be praised: so shall I be saved from mine enemies.*

Conclusion

_____

_____

_____

Study Questions

1. What was David's initial response to his trial with Saul?

2. Read 1 Samuel 30:1–6. David was still enduring a great trial and had just experienced defeat at the hand of the Amalekites, yet what did he do in 1 Samuel 30:6?

3. Think of a trial you may have experienced in the past or perhaps are enduring now. Explain how you handled or are handling your trial and identify key moments when you encouraged yourself in the Lord. If you have not found rest in the Lord, spend a moment now to encourage yourself in Him.

4. Explain David's lapse as recorded in 2 Samuel 11:1.

5. While David's trial dealt with his relationship to Saul, whom did his temptation involve?

6. What should a Christian do when faced with temptation?

7. Look up the following verses and list the consequences David experienced as a result of his sin:

> 2 Samuel 12:15–16
>
> 2 Samuel 13:1–12
>
> 2 Samuel 13:29
>
> 2 Samuel 18:10–12

8. What did David do to experience triumph after his temptation?

Memory Verse

1 CORINTHIANS 10:13

13 *There hath no temptation taken you but such as is common to man: but God is faithful, who will not suffer you to be tempted above that ye are able; but will with the temptation also make a way to escape, that ye may be able to bear it.*

The Journey to the Cross

Key Verses
John 17

Lesson Overview
The most significant journey recorded in the Bible is the journey to the Cross. Jesus' journey to Golgotha was incredibly personal and painful. Yet His journey was wonderfully powerful, as He ultimately conquered death and the grave in an expression of love for mankind. This power is still changing lives today.

As Christians, we must constantly examine our lives in light of Bible truth. By considering the people and events surrounding Jesus' death on the Cross, we can develop an understanding of the significance of Jesus' death, burial, and resurrection. We must evaluate our spiritual journeys in light of these truths, beginning with the confidence of salvation and continuing forward in a life of righteous living.

Lesson Aim
We must realize that if Christ died for us, we should accept His gift of salvation and then determine to live our lives in a way that would glorify Him.

Introduction

_____

_____

_____

I. A _____ Journey

A. A _____ *journey*

JOHN 1:1–2

1   In the beginning was the Word, and the Word was with God, and the Word was God.

2   The same was in the beginning with God.

1 PETER 1:18–20

18   Forasmuch as ye know that ye were not redeemed with corruptible things, as silver and gold, from your vain conversation received by tradition from your fathers;

19   But with the precious blood of Christ, as of a lamb without blemish and without spot:

20   Who verily was foreordained before the foundation of the world, but was manifest in these last times for you,

B. A _____ *journey*

1 JOHN 5:20

20   And we know that the Son of God is come, and hath given us an understanding, that we may know him that is true, and we are in him that is true, even in his Son Jesus Christ. This is the true God, and eternal life.

1 CORINTHIANS 6:20

20   For ye are bought with a price: therefore glorify God in your body, and in your spirit, which are God's.

II. A _____ Journey

A. Personal _____

JOHN 18:1

1   When Jesus had spoken these words, he went forth with his disciples over the brook Cedron, where was a garden, into the which he entered, and his disciples.

JOHN 18:5

5   They answered him, Jesus of Nazareth. Jesus saith unto them, I am he. And Judas also, which betrayed him, stood with them.

MATTHEW 26:48

48   Now he that betrayed him gave them a sign, saying, Whomsoever I shall kiss, that same is he: hold him fast.

JOHN 18:17–18

17   Then saith the damsel that kept the door unto Peter, Art not thou also one of this man's disciples? He saith, I am not.

18   And the servants and officers stood there, who had made a fire of coals; for it was cold: and they warmed themselves: and Peter stood with them, and warmed himself.

B. Physical _____

JOHN 19:1–4

1   Then Pilate therefore took Jesus, and scourged him.

2   And the soldiers platted a crown of thorns, and put it on his head, and they put on him a purple robe,

3   And said, Hail, King of the Jews! And they smote him with their hands.

4   Pilate therefore went forth again, and saith unto them, Behold, I bring him forth to you, that ye may know that I find no fault in him.

JOHN 18:38

38   Pilate saith unto him, What is truth? And when he had said this, he went out again unto the Jews, and saith unto them, I find in him no fault at all.

III. A _____ Journey

JOHN 19:17–21

17   And he bearing his cross went forth into a place called the place of a skull, which is called in the Hebrew Golgotha:

18   Where they crucified him, and two other with him, on either side one, and Jesus in the midst.

19   And Pilate wrote a title, and put it on the cross. And the writing was, JESUS OF NAZARETH THE KING OF THE JEWS.

20   This title then read many of the Jews: for the place where Jesus was crucified was nigh to the city: and it was written in Hebrew, and Greek, and Latin.

21   Then said the chief priests of the Jews to Pilate, Write not, The King of the Jews; but that he said, I am King of the Jews.

A. *The power of* _____

ROMANS 5:6–8

6   For when we were yet without strength, in due time Christ died for the ungodly.

7   For scarcely for a righteous man will one die: yet peradventure for a good man some would even dare to die.

8   But God commendeth his love toward us, in that, while we were yet sinners, Christ died for us.

JOHN 15:13

13   Greater love hath no man than this, that a man lay down his life for his friends.

EPHESIANS 5:2

2   And walk in love, as Christ also hath loved us, and hath given himself for us an offering and a sacrifice to God for a sweetsmelling savour.

B. *The power of* _____

ISAIAH 53:12

12   Therefore will I divide him a portion with the great, and he shall divide the spoil with the strong; because he hath poured out his soul unto death: and he was numbered with the transgressors; and he bare the sin of many, and made intercession for the transgressors.

LUKE 23:34

34   Then said Jesus, Father, forgive them; for they know not what they do. And they parted his raiment, and cast lots.

C. *The power of* _____

JOHN 19:30

30 When Jesus therefore had received the vinegar, he said, It is finished: and he bowed his head, and gave up the ghost.

Conclusion

MATTHEW 12:40

40 For as Jonas was three days and three nights in the whale's belly; so shall the Son of man be three days and three nights in the heart of the earth.

ROMANS 1:16

16 For I am not ashamed of the gospel of Christ: for it is the power of God unto salvation to every one that believeth; to the Jew first, and also to the Greek.

Study Questions

1. What is the definition of omniscient?

2. How was the journey to the Cross personal for Jesus?

3. What was the first and main purpose of Jesus' death on the Cross?

4. In addition to offering salvation, what other purpose did Jesus' death on the Cross serve?

5. Write out 1 Corinthians 6:20, and list two specific ways in which you can glorify God this week.

6. From whom did Jesus experience personal betrayal?

7. List three practical ways in which you can "stand with Jesus" in a world that denies Him.

8. How did Jesus display humility from the Cross?

Memory Verse

2 CORINTHIANS 5:15

15 *And that he died for all, that they which live should not henceforth live unto themselves, but unto him which died for them, and rose again.*

The Journey to the Tomb

Key Verses

Luke 24:1–8

Lesson Overview

Jesus died on the Cross and, for His followers, all hope died with Him. He was placed in a tomb, and the tomb was sealed. The crucifixion was the ultimate of shattered dreams. There would be no kingdom. There would be no king. After days of mourning, Mary Magdalene, Mary the mother of Jesus, and other ladies were making a journey to the tomb to pay their last respects to the One in whom they had placed all of their hope. When they arrived, the stone was rolled away and two angels appeared to them proclaiming the news that Jesus had risen. Bewildered, they ran to tell Jesus' disciples the wonderful news.

Lesson Aim

By examining the events surrounding the burial and resurrection of Christ, we should seek to understand that as we claim the promises of God and practice the presence of Christ, He can turn sorrow into joy on our journeys of faith, and transform us in the process!

Introduction

_____

_____

_____

JOHN 19:16–19

16 Then delivered he him therefore unto them to be crucified. And they took Jesus, and led him away.

17 And he bearing his cross went forth into a place called the place of a skull, which is called in the Hebrew Golgotha:

18 Where they crucified him, and two other with him, on either side one, and Jesus in the midst.

19 And Pilate wrote a title, and put it on the cross. And the writing was, JESUS OF NAZARETH THE KING OF THE JEWS.

I. A _____ Journey

MARK 16:10

10 And she went and told them that had been with him, as they mourned and wept.

A. _____ the Saviour's death

LUKE 8:2

2 And certain women, which had been healed of evil spirits and infirmities, Mary called Magdalene, out of whom went seven devils,

B. _____ by the empty tomb

JOHN 20:1–4

1 The first day of the week cometh Mary Magdalene early, when it was yet dark, unto the sepulchre, and seeth the stone taken away from the sepulchre.

2   Then she runneth, and cometh to Simon Peter, and to the other disciple, whom Jesus loved, and saith unto them, They have taken away the Lord out of the sepulchre, and we know not where they have laid him.

3   Peter therefore went forth, and that other disciple, and came to the sepulchre.

4   So they ran both together: and the other disciple did outrun Peter, and came first to the sepulchre.

JOHN 2:19

19   Jesus answered and said unto them, Destroy this temple, and in three days I will raise it up.

MATTHEW 26:31–32

31   Then saith Jesus unto them, All ye shall be offended because of me this night: for it is written, I will smite the shepherd, and the sheep of the flock shall be scattered abroad.

32   But after I am risen again, I will go before you into Galilee.

II. A _____ Journey

A. *Their fears were* _____

LUKE 24:36–39

36   And as they thus spake, Jesus himself stood in the midst of them, and saith unto them, Peace be unto you.

37   But they were terrified and affrighted, and supposed that they had seen a spirit.

38   And he said unto them, Why are ye troubled? and why do thoughts arise in your hearts?

39   Behold my hands and my feet, that it is I myself: handle me, and see; for a spirit hath not flesh and bones, as ye see me have.

B. Their sorrow was _____

III. A _____ **Journey**

A. *Transformed through _____*

MARK 14:66–72

66   And as Peter was beneath in the palace, there cometh one of the maids of the high priest:

67   And when she saw Peter warming himself, she looked upon him, and said, And thou also wast with Jesus of Nazareth.

68   But he denied, saying, I know not, neither understand I what thou sayest. And he went out into the porch; and the cock crew.

69   And a maid saw him again, and began to say to them that stood by, This is one of them.

70   And he denied it again. And a little after, they that stood by said again to Peter, Surely thou art one of them: for thou art a Galilaean, and thy speech agreeth thereto.

71   But he began to curse and to swear, saying, I know not this man of whom ye speak.

72   And the second time the cock crew. And Peter called to mind the word that Jesus said unto him, Before the cock crow twice, thou shalt deny me thrice. And when he thought thereon, he wept.

MARK 16:6–7

6   And he saith unto them, Be not affrighted: Ye seek Jesus of Nazareth, which was crucified: he is risen; he is not here: behold the place where they laid him.

7   But go your way, tell his disciples and Peter that he goeth before you into Galilee: there shall ye see him, as he said unto you.

1 JOHN 1:9

9   *If we confess our sins, he is faithful and just to forgive us our sins, and to cleanse us from all unrighteousness.*

B.   *Transformed through* _____

JOHN 20:24–29

24   *But Thomas, one of the twelve, called Didymus, was not with them when Jesus came.*

25   *The other disciples therefore said unto him, We have seen the Lord. But he said unto them, Except I shall see in his hands the print of the nails, and put my finger into the print of the nails, and thrust my hand into his side, I will not believe.*

26   *And after eight days again his disciples were within, and Thomas with them: then came Jesus, the doors being shut, and stood in the midst, and said, Peace be unto you.*

27   *Then saith he to Thomas, Reach hither thy finger, and behold my hands; and reach hither thy hand, and thrust it into my side: and be not faithless, but believing.*

28   *And Thomas answered and said unto him, My Lord and my God.*

29   *Jesus saith unto him, Thomas, because thou hast seen me, thou hast believed:* **blessed are they that have not seen, and yet have believed.**

JOHN 11:25

25   *Jesus said unto her, I am the resurrection, and the life: he that believeth in me, though he were dead, yet shall he live:*

1 CORINTHIANS 15:19–20

19   *If in this life only we have hope in Christ, we are of all men most miserable.*

20   *But now is Christ risen from the dead, and become the firstfruits of them that slept.*

Conclusion

_____

_____

_____

JOHN 14:1–6

1   *Let not your heart be troubled: ye believe in God, believe also in me.*

2   *In my Father's house are many mansions: if it were not so, I would have told you. I go to prepare a place for you.*

3   *And if I go and prepare a place for you, I will come again, and receive you unto myself; that where I am, there ye may be also.*

4   *And whither I go ye know, and the way ye know.*

5   *Thomas saith unto him, Lord, we know not whither thou goest; and how can we know the way?*

6   *Jesus saith unto him, I am the way, the truth, and the life: no man cometh unto the Father, but by me.*

Study Questions

1. What is the one obvious difference between the death of Jesus and the death of other religious leaders and humans throughout the world?

2. Explain how God had worked in Mary Magdelene's life prior to her journey to the tomb.

3. Name two ways our fears can be relieved.

4. Give one reference that proves Jesus had promised He would rise again.

5. List three ways you can remember the words and promises of God.

6. When God forgives, He receives us back into fellowship with Himself. Look up Psalm 103:2–4 and list the four actions performed by God, proving His complete forgiveness.

7. What is the ultimate transformation that can take place in our lives because of the death and resurrection of Jesus?

8. Take a moment to think of the fears or sorrows you are facing in your life right now. List two promises (including Scripture references) you can claim from God's Word to help you experience the joy Jesus offers.

Memory Verse
JOHN 11:25
25 Jesus said unto her, I am the resurrection, and the life: he that believeth in me, though he were dead, yet shall he live:

For additional Christian
growth resources visit
www.strivingtogether.com